Can You Dye Your Thoughts In My Ink?

How to get lost and link your thoughts in
My Ink?

Shambhavi Umesh

BookLeaf
Publishing

India | USA | UK

Made with ❤ on the BookLeaf Publishing Platform
www.bookleafpub.in
www.bookleafpub.com

Dedication

To **all my people, my reviewers, the random readers and their positive comments** on my writings which actually motivated me to come up with this poetry, which definitely traverses you all through many of your lines of life journey and relates them, brushes them up and feel refreshed afresh. Your dedicated support and love for poetry is much appreciated and valued. **A heartfelt thanks to all those buddies.**

Preface

After being continuously involved in drilling my brain and dirtying hands to ink, I was always being pushed by a curiosity of launching my own book. Yes! The same hunger has landed me here today to **"Write one & My First One"**. The first reason of writing this book **"Can You Dye Your Thoughts in My Ink?"** is to have reader's attention on day to day emotions in oneself like the love towards the mother, handling a bold father, giggling laughters, funny gossips, gracious smiles, debate between people, raged fights, draught sadness, the stress life, experiencing the introverts and the deadly extroverts, anonymous helping hands & their hospitality, budding feelings, disappointments, importance of self love etc., in a quite poetic way which amuses you, outcome being **"A WIDER AND A BROADER SMILE"** as I always believe **"Live to Cure, Not to hurt"**.

Acknowledgements

I acknowledge and appreciate each of you below:

- I would dedicate my primary acknowledgement to My Lovely God, **"Sri Krishna"**, the almighty who has blessed me with the art of expressing and connecting the people's heart and soul right together.

- Post Almighty, I would like to be thankful to my **Guru Santhosh ji** , who is a mighty support for all my optimistic thoughts in life. Thank You Anna (brother).

- Secondly, I would love to thank my parents **Mr. Umesh(Seenanna) & Mrs. Rajani S S(Radha)** who always say, ***"Hey! You write well and I get Connected***'. Especially, My mom has read my quotes and poems on Lord Sri Krishna written in my Mother Tongue i.e., Kannada. Trust me, She loves it.

- A heartful thanks to **Padmashree, Chandini & Razia Sultana** for being kind enough to review and provide feedback for my work **"Can You Dye Your Thoughts in My Ink?"** .I Owe you For it. Thank a lot as It means a lot.

- Also, I would thank **My Readers** who are my best buddies, my lovely friends, beloved family, extended family, my supportive colleagues and obviously my random readers for their positive comments on my writings.

All of you have motivated me knowingly or unknowingly to execute and come up with this poetry which definitely traverses you through some of your phases in life or lines to relate your voyage of a past, present and future.

Your dedicated support and love for poetry is much appreciated and I am thankful for that.

Daughter's First Prince 'PAPPA'

PAPPA, When I was born, You were just off the door,
When You were permitted in, You rushed in, to shower a
joyful pour.
Constantly soothing, Consistently comforting to adore,
Excellent! Unfailingly, You are always there as a
hardcore,
Just right before, to bestow more and more, also still
more.

PAPPA, With my tiny hands as a powerful gear,
I gently started to crawl, I see! You were right on the
floor,
Solely, to sense the miniature vibes, sightsee my cute
little-tour,
Gradually, I grew up, And One day I babbled,
'Appappappapa....',
Wow! No Doubt, Your Smile Inclined so high, to touch
the Sky.

PAPPA, I recall, I was cheered up to sing on the shore,
Abruptly, You pushed me on to the floor.
Trust me! I was fearing, screaming and doubting myself
to score,
Back the stage, 'The Stout You', seemed very loud to roar,
Yay! I filled in all the air from within, to lead myself to
dare,
Performing and competing with all the power like never
before,
You poured your might Confidence in me, destined to
reach the core,
Like never before and like never after!

A 'MOM' To Be

A Mom to be, is a Challenging to be,
A Mom to be, is a Blessing to be,
A Mom to be, is surely not a Tiring to be.

A Mom to be, is not at all a Burden to be,
A Mom to be, is not like a 'Cool Father' may be!
But, She is always there for you, as a need to be.

A Mom to be, is not what she wanted to be,
Have You ever asked her in life? What she had to be?
Have You ever questioned her? Is this the way she is
meant to be?
Have You ever wondered? Is she really Deemed to be?
In a hushed tone, mumbles a 'No' from within,
"What a pity? She is just what we all have Formed her to
be" Isn't it?

Drama Queen, No Better than Your BFF

Exceptionally, Out from that Universe,
Extremely, Out from Nowhere,
Just Out from that Comfort Jar,
Awfully, Out like a twinkling star!
Whoo! There, Comes my bestie!
From a pathway, remarkably very far,
Why? Is it just to repair my dark scar?

Hey, Her actions have no bar,
Hey, Her acting's have no avatar,
Hey, Her behaviors resembles an actor,
But, Believe Me! She is the only one to widely pamper.

Unknowingly she acts and Unwillingly she asks,
In Contrast, Knowingly she asks and Willingly she acts!
Trust Me! She manages both in equal scales,
For no-one to point a little and dare!

I own her, I owe her,

I like her, I dislike her,
My Bestie, My Rules!
Hey Listen, She is not at all an option,
Yay! She is "MY CHOICE, OUT OF PRIDE"!

'Bro' is just not a 'Bro'

Bro, is Just Not a Bro,
In the beginning, My Bro, will be my Toaster,
Gradually, He turns out to be my Roaster!
And Finally, He becomes my BP Booster.
Yes, Correct! Bro is Just Not a Bro.

Though He never appreciates me from earlier,
For all my regards and honor,
Unexpectedly, He becomes my boaster!
As he feels I am the best Coffee Maker to honor,
Hope, He recognizes me sooner or never later.

In his Phantom, I may not look in good flavor,
But, I always plead almighty in his favor,
Just trying to be his second Mother,
Always adoring my Naughty Brother.
Bro, is Just Not a Bro,
He is a highly rated Pro,
And, He is my one and only Little Bro.

Introvert & A Deadly Extrovert

An Introvert says a 'Hello' after a month/an year,
An Extrovert says a lot within a minute or a second.

An Introvert is more binded by himself/herself
An Extrovert surrounds himself/herself by all the Crowd.

An Introvert probably doesn't get tempted by a spotlight
An Extrovert is on his/her toes to get well spotted.

An Introvert hates Socialism, as it drains him/her
Contrastly, An Extrovert loves this subject, just not to
drain themselves!

An Introvert Cries on the biggest sorrows to heal, just by
himself/herself!
In Contrary Fashion, An Extrovert needs Big scene to
Console on just a tender wound!

Trust Me! An Introvert Works better on their own,

But! Extroverts mostly Work better in group/troop!

You are Unique being an Introvert or A Deadly
Extrovert,
Light up Your Essence and Flavors to brighten Yourself,
And to Qualify the Virtue of Yourself!

Carrying a Load? Drop it

Are you carrying the load too Much?
Are you holding the load for someone's Clutch?
Are you tightly hanging on the load to avoid the flush?
Or Are you possessing your load, just not allow it to
crush?

I know it may be a personnel load, yet painful,
I know it may be a professional workload, very strainful,
Come-On ! It may also be a lazy load! And it's Awful!

Drop it to reduce the burden,
Drop it to decrease the stress,
Drop it to suppress the obsess,
And Drop it to start your own Chess!
On a finishing touch, Drop it,
To encode Yourself to decode again!

Why Debate? Just Conclude

In the beginning, Debate kicks off as a Healthy Start,
Fewer steps further, pros and cons from ends start a tug
of war,
Later, the war breaks out and turns out unhealthy,
Ha Ha! Finally, You both have lost tracks, As None
Agree!

No-one to stop, you rage on each other,
No-one to drop, it continues. Neither to defend nor to
defeat,
Equal scales it goes on and on,
Your throat dries off, looks for a chilled water,
Then You cool just for a pause!

Many debates end up without Conclusions,
But with lot of Confusions, leading to grudges.
Break the Ice, Share the outcomes,
Not that you are less, but to seek more.
Why Debate? Can't We Soon Conclude?
Why Debate? Quickly, Just Conclude!

Try To Weep, than to hide

Come out of the, burried darkness,
Come out of the, hidden insights,
Come out of the, cozy loneliness,
Come out of the, cover that bothers,
Come out of the, invisibility that haunts,
I Plead You! Please Come out to never forget your
flaunts!

I agree, the pain is harsh,
I agree, the hurt is a huge crash,
I agree, the burn is aching the rash,
I Know, You have masked your tears,
And never allowed its rush !

Do not Hide! Weep away all your pains,
Do not Hide! Wipe off, those haunting scars,
Do not Hide! Sweep away the tear,
Do not Hide! Rip off those masked tears,
Do not Hide! Just Sweep and Weep, Louder and Much
Louder!

Fix It ASAP

Life may have bundle of issues,
Life may have queue of problems,
Life may leave you lonely in a disaster,
Life may treat you like an unknown child,
Life may unequally portray you!
Life may knowingly or unknowingly stamp you hard!

Be ready to deal with it,
Be steady to meddle it,
Be ready to swallow it,
Be ready to throw it,
Be awakened to bury it,
Just Be Ready to Fix it ASAP!

Does Humanity Still Exists?

I was out on a Showery day,
I was out on a light Drizzly day,
I was out on that early Wetty day,
I was out to commute to kick off my Weekday.

I was fixing myself to get off my transport,
To My Amuse! I bumped in disappointment!
My brain kicked off very tight,
Alas! Now I see Why and What?
Ouch! I have Neither an Umbrella to Rain shade nor a
Canopy to Shelter at!

I grasped and grinned to utmost, to set myself to the
shower,
I moved like a Tiny Chick which lost its Mother,
I drove myself to comfort and alarming myself to avoid a
troll.

All of a Sudden! A human of thirty's walked by me and
exclaimed,

"Hey, Young Lady! Why are you drenching in rain?,
Just Come-On and Join in, Just don't get too drained".

I really wondered! Does Humanity Still Exists?
Besides and further, Does Humanity do even persist?
Deeper to the context, In case a metricist measures and a
jurist judges,
It results in a truthfulness to whitelist, At the utter top
digits!
Yes! To Cheer, Boost & Uplift , Humanity Co-exists!
Whoo! Humanity Naturally do exists & Genuinely Pre-
Exists!

Believe! My Pet Cured Me

My Pet, a tiny little Kiddo,
My Pet, a high power packet,
My Pet, impatient to another level,
My Pet, especially keen and restless to higher extent,
To experience the world in all the sense, also in his
sense!

Early Morning, He eagerly waits out the door, to rush
indoors,
To Pamper me and Drag me off the cozy couch,
Before the Sun rise, He wakes himself up,
Just like a scheduled alarm, To Welcome The Sun,
And To Welcome His Loved ones!

Mom, wakes up afresh and steps to the door,
Poor fellow, Yet waiting for the open door,
As soon as she freed the door wide open,
He passionately runs onto my bunk,
To wake me up, like a strict warden of mine,
He drags off, scrapes off my sheets,

Alas! As always, I resist to wakeup and wave,
He, Failing to pull me off, adjusts himself next to me!
To just go crazy and fancy over my cuddles and pampers.
Awww! He is such a Little Cute Baby!

He gets annoyed when I don't converse with him,
He gets hyperactive when I just sign on him for a game,
He is always there for a nap on my lap when I am down,
He is more alive when I am happier,
Trust Me! He keeps me awake and lively,
In a way around, He cured me mentally!
To escape from all the Traumas of Sadness
My Pet is always the one for me,
Believe Me! My Pet Completely Cured Me.

No Expectations, Zero Scars

When You Intend a lot , You Tear down a lot,
When You Expect More, Be Ready to deal it's Hurt even
more,
When You Expect too much, You end up being slapped
very very much,
When Bigger promises are made, darker anxieties
shadows its shade,
Hey! There are High chances, Remember! It results in
extra bitterness,
Too much Loved You are Today! Never Know, It may not
even exist another day!

Tie yourself not to expect More,
Free Yourself to just foresee less,
Fewer lists and Minor twists, Isn't it?
Limited schedules, Lesser declines! Isn't it?
Start a Marathon to jog on lesser Expectations,
It's Here You Rejuvenate and Rise Again,
It's then, Your Small Moves, forms your Smile wider,
And all the minute Graphs that incline,

You destine to shine! Just like a Red Wine!
Am I Too Honest? No Expectations, Zero Scars? Yes or
No? You Conclude!

With Hopes, Fill Your Heart

Doubt is something that ruins you from within,
Doubt is something that drowns you in,
Doubt is something that traps you to spin and spin,
No Doubt! No Doubt! Now You Do Not Doubt to win.

Tender Your Heart to act smart,
Tender Your Heart, not to Doubt your start.
Tender Your Heart, to Believe in your own chart,
Not Tough ! Not Tough ! This is all what it takes to Kick-
start.

With Hatred, Do Not Fill Your Heart,
With Pain, Do Not Stuff Your Heart,
With Sorrow, Do not satisfy Your Heart,
Hey, To Know your Ropes, Just Fill Your Heart,
Exactly, Wholly With all the Hopes, Fill Your Heart.

Pause, But Resume

You need to Pause to discontinue,
You need to Pause to later Continue,
You need to Pause to self review for a 'New You',
Guess what? You Need it just for You, You and You!

Pause to breathe in the fresh air,
Pause to breathe out the dirty tear,
Come On, Let the whole world rudely stare,
No Matter, Just Pause and Push on to rarely dare.

Not to resist, Not to persist the longer pause,
Drag in all the spirit to, unmute the muted clause.
Resume yourself from within for a true cause.
Yes! Just Resume to Become your own Boss!
Again Not to Pause & Toss Or Toss & Again Pause!

Laughs & Giggles, To Fill You

Laugh aloud to calm down,
Laugh aloud not to drown,
Giggle for no reason, but to trigger you,
Chuckle for sometime, to motivate you.

Burst out Your laughter, With no other Choice,
Roar your laughter to know Your Noise,
Dare the Smiles with People unknown,
Cheer Your Laughs with People Very known.

Crack out to be the weird funniest,
Don't grin, laugh to the fullest,
Don't break up, burst out to the deepest,
Laugh & Giggle, To Fill You & Fill You Deep.

Gather the Pieces into 'PEACE'

You may be hurt by a little cut,
Less it aches, More it resonates,
You may be defeated by an emotional battle,
Trust Me! It digs a pothole deeper to misery,
More it aches, Further it bleeds.

It may be the deeper cramps, never allow you to decide,
Or, It may be a cut piece, proceeding to further cut you
inside.

Glue your trashes into PEACE,
Glue your fragments into PEACE,
Glue your bits and pieces into PEACE,
Go Ahead! Gather all Your Pieces into "THE PEACE"!
Agree?

Thank You! Means a Lot

Thank Your Mother for all the load she carried,
Thank Your Father for all the boldness he showcased,
Thank Your Guru for discovering a readable version of
You.
Thank Your Siblings for all the craziness they posses.
Else, You would definitely have missed all the fun,
Also, Thank Your Children for adding an essence to your
journey.
And, Thank Your Grand Parents for their Endless Care.

Thank Your Well-Wisher who resumed you out from that
pause & streamed you off the reach,
Thank Your Bestie for all that she dealt being your
buddy,
Thank Your Co-Worker for always showed up for you,
Thank Your Neighbors for being present in your absence,

Thank Your laborer for being on duty each day,
Thank Your Doctor for all the Cure,
Thank Your Readers for all their time,

Thank Your Viewers for all their bigtime,
Thank You! A Heartfelt Gesture & Heart filled Comment,
It's a Big Remark,
Definitely! Thank You, Means a Lot! Means a Lot for
Everyone!

Post Your Life Trek is, 'A Beautiful Viewpoint'

Rewind your life pages back,
Unwind the happy moments,
Unwind the cheerless sorrows,
Remind Yourself With all the Struggles,
Unbind Yourself With all your Pasts.

Don't You grasp that the climbs had depressed you so
high?
And, Don't You think that slopes had motivated you
high?
Don't You exclaim that Surrounding greens had pushed
you front in Your Life Trek?
Don't You realize, Your Life, It's a Wonderful Trek?

Being Unhappy all through the journey,
Being depressed when you paused and doubted,
Being Pessimistic about reaching your destiny,
Finally, you have reached the destination of your life
Trek,

More Amused You Are , Much Satisfied Your Are,
To Witness Where Your Journey has led You To,
In Fact, its a mesmerized excitement and pleasure,
Trust Me! Post Your Life Trek is, 'A Beautiful Viewpoint'!
To Turn Back & Exclaim!